What Are Solids, Liquids, and Gases?

Exploring Science with Hands-on Activities

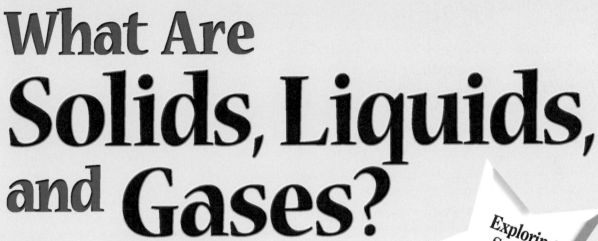

Richard and Louise Spilsbury

Enslow Elementary
an imprint of
Enslow Publishers, Inc.
40 Industrial Road
Box 398
Berkeley Heights, NJ 07922
USA

http://www.enslow.com

Enslow Elementary, an imprint of Enslow Publishers, Inc.

Enslow Elementary® is a registered trademark of Enslow Publishers, Inc.

This edition published in 2008 by Enslow Publishers, Inc.

Library of Congress Cataloging-in-Publication Data

Spilsbury, Richard, 1963-
  What are solids, liquids, and gases? : exploring science with hands-on activities / Richard and Louise Spilsbury.
     p. cm. — (In touch with basic science)
  Summary: "A beginners look at the states of matter for third and fourth grades"—Provided by publisher.
  Includes bibliographical references and index.
  ISBN-13: 978-0-7660-3094-7
  ISBN-10: 0-7660-3094-6
  1. Matter—Properties—Experiments—Juvenile literature.
2. Science—Experiments—Juvenile literature. 3. Science—Study and teaching—Activity programs—Juvenile literature. I. Spilsbury, Louise. II. Title.
  QC173.36.S655 2008
  530.4078—dc22

                              2007024516

Printed in the United States of America

10 9 8 7 6 5 4 3 2 1

For The Brown Reference Group plc
Project Editor: Sarah Eason
Designer: Paul Myerscough
Picture Researcher: Maria Joannou
Managing Editor: Bridget Giles
Editorial Director: Lindsey Lowe
Production Director: Alastair Gourlay
Children's Publisher: Anne O'Daly

Photographic and Illustration Credits: Illustrations by Geoff Ward. Model Photography by Tudor Photography. Additional photographs from istockphoto, pp. 4, 6, 9, 14, 24; Rex Features/Jennifer Jacquemart , p. 20; Shutterstock, p. 8.

Cover Photo: Tudor Photography

contents

Inside Matter **4**

States of Matter **6**

Solids **8**

Cutting and Shaping 10

Disappearing Solids 12

Liquids **14**

Mixing Liquids 16

Creating Bubbles 18

Gases **20**

Expanding Gases 22

Changing States **24**

Vapor Trails 26

Sliding Ice 28

Glossary **30**

Further Reading **31**

Index **32**

INSIDE MATTER

Everything in the universe is made of matter, from the smallest drop of water to the largest skyscrapers and the stars in the sky.

All matter is made of parts that we cannot see. These parts are called atoms. People often call atoms "the building blocks of matter." Just as a big house is made of many small bricks, every substance is made of millions of atoms.

Atoms are incredibly small. More than a billion atoms would fit inside just one period on this page!

What Are Molecules?

Atoms do not usually exist alone. They are often joined to other atoms. Two or more joined atoms are called a molecule. Some molecules are made up of only one type of atom, while others include more than one type.

CLOSE-UP

THE PARTS OF AN ATOM

The center of an atom is called a nucleus. It is made of protons and neutrons joined by a strong force, called a nuclear force. Protons have a positive electrical charge and neutrons are neutral—they have no electrical charge. Tiny electrons outside the nucleus have small negative electrical charges. A positive charge attracts a negative charge, which is why electrons move around the nucleus.

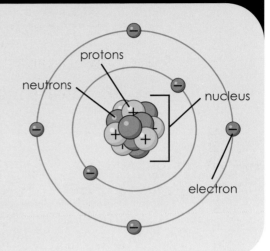

◄ *Around 100 different types of atoms have been found. These atoms combine into molecules in millions of different ways and amounts to form everything around us.*

Some molecules contain a few atoms, while others contain many.

Molecules that contain millions of atoms are still incredibly tiny. There are billions of molecules in just one spoonful of sugar.

Inside an Atom

Inside each atom are even tinier particles called protons, neutrons, and electrons. Different kinds of atoms contain different numbers of protons, neutrons, and electrons. However, a single atom of any kind usually has the same number of protons as electrons.

STATES OF MATTER

Matter comes in different forms, including liquids, solids, and gases. For example, a brick is solid, water is liquid, and the air around us is a gas. Solid, liquid, and gas are called "states of matter."

Solid

A substance that has a fixed shape is called a solid. A solid object, such as a rock, does not change shape because its atoms and molecules are joined in a tight, regular pattern.

Liquid

A liquid is a substance that does not have a fixed shape. It flows or pours. If water is poured into a tray, the water spreads out and covers the bottom of the tray. The molecules in a liquid are packed closely together. They are not bonded as tightly as the molecules in a solid, so they can move around.

Gas

A gas spreads out in all directions and does not have a fixed shape. Gas cannot be poured into a tray—it will float away and spread out in the air. When gas is put into a closed jar, the gas spreads out to fill the whole jar. The molecules in a gas are spaced out and do not have a regular pattern.

◄ *The three different states of matter can be seen in this picture. The bottle is a solid, liquid is contained inside the bottle, and the bubbles are filled with a gas—air.*

CLOSE-UP

ARRANGING MOLECULES

The molecules inside a solid are packed closely together and usually arranged in a regular pattern.

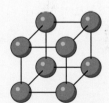

The molecules inside a liquid are also packed closely together. They are not arranged in a regular pattern.

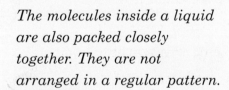

The molecules inside a gas are widely spaced. They are not joined to each other and are always moving.

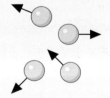

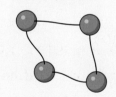

SOLIDS

There are many different types of solids. Some are soft and others are hard. Some are rigid and others are flexible.

The atoms and molecules of solids are held together by pulling forces called bonds. A solid's hardness depends on how strong these bonds are. Hard solids, such as diamonds, have strong bonds.

▲ *The molecules of diamonds are held together by extremely strong bonds. That makes diamonds very hard.*

Stretching Solids

Some solids can be stretched a little. That is because their atoms and molecules can be pulled further away from each other than normal. When the solid is released, the bonds between its atoms and molecules become tight again, and the solid returns to its original shape.

If a solid is stretched too far, its bonds break. For example, a sheet of plastic can be bent a little but will break if it is bent too much.

CLOSE-UP

DISSOLVING

Solid grains of sugar dissolve in water because the molecules in water gradually pull away molecules from the sugar grains. Each sugar grain may break into individual molecules, which spread evenly in the spaces between the water molecules.

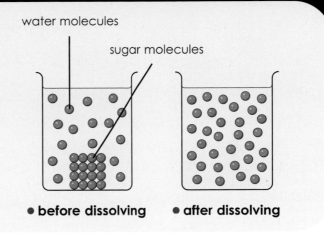

water molecules

sugar molecules

● **before dissolving**   ● **after dissolving**

▲ *Seawater contains dissolved salt. Some of the salt in seawater comes from salt in rocks and mud on the ocean floor.*

Cutting and Shaping Solids

A solid has a fixed volume. It always takes up the same amount of space. One way to change a solid's shape is to cut or break it. There are many different tools for cutting and shaping different solids. For instance, scissors will cut paper, but a saw is needed to cut through wood.

Dissolving

Some solid substances, such as sugar, dissolve when mixed with a liquid. The solid breaks into pieces so tiny we cannot see them. When sugar dissolves in water, the water looks clear. But we know the sugar is still there because the water tastes sweet. A liquid in which something has dissolved is called a solution.

9

Cutting and Shaping

Can you cut a potato with a straw? Can you shape flour with your fingers? Try these activities!

1 Try to cut off a piece of potato using the long, smooth side of the straw. Now put your thumb over one end of the straw. Stab the other end into the potato. What happens?

You will need

- plastic straw • raw potato • piece of wood • a piece of rough sandpaper
- a piece of smooth sandpaper
- thread • a small piece of clay
- 1/4 cup of water • 1 cup of all-purpose flour • bowl • 1/4 cup of salt

2 Rub the wood with different types of sandpaper. Which one makes the wood smoothest? Which one shapes the wood fastest?

3 Wrap the thread around a piece of clay. Pull the loop of thread tight to cut the clay.

10

4 Put the flour into the bowl. Use your fingers to try to make the flour into a shape. What happens?

5 Mix the salt, water, and flour to make dough. Shape the dough. Have an adult put it into a warm oven at 375°F for 20 minutes. Does the dough keep its shape?

SAFETY TIP

Ask an adult to light the oven and lift the dough in and out.

WHAT HAPPENED?

Cutting

The smooth side of the straw could not cut the potato. The sharper end of the straw cut the potato a little. The thread cut the clay because its edges were as thin and sharp as a knife.

Shaping

Sandpaper has pieces of grit on its surface. The rough sandpaper had bigger pieces of grit, which is why it shaped the wood faster. The smoother sandpaper had smoother pieces of grit and made the wood smoother.

When you added water to the flour, it made its starch molecules sticky. That held the flour together. The water evaporated when you put the dough in the oven, and it became hard.

11

Disappearing Solids

Some solids disappear when they are added to a liquid. Follow the steps below to discover why.

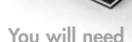

You will need
- large measuring cup • water
- cup and saucer • notebook
- pen • thermometer (the type used for taking body temperature)
- sugar • teaspoon • hot water

1 Fill the measuring cup to the 16 oz (500 ml) mark with cold water. Use some of this water to fill the cup up to the top. Use the amount of water left in the measuring cup to figure out how much water went into the cup.

2 Slide the thermometer into the cup. Write down the temperature of the water.

3 Carefully sprinkle a teaspoon of sugar into the cup of water. Wait for the sugar to dissolve. Then carefully add more sugar, one spoonful at a time.

4 Stop adding sugar when the water starts to spill over the side of the cup. Write down the number of spoonfuls of sugar you added to the water.

5 Repeat this experiment with hot water. What happens?

Try this!

Try this experiment again, but this time use a spoon to stir the sugar into the cold and hot water. You should find the sugar dissolves more quickly when the water is stirred. Stirring helps spread the molecules of the solid (sugar) through the liquid (water), so the sugar molecules move more quickly into spaces among the liquid molecules.

WHAT HAPPENED?

More spoonfuls of sugar dissolved in the hot water than the cold water. As molecules move, the spaces between them become larger. The molecules in hot water move more than the molecules in cold water. That is because hot water has more heat energy. The heat energy broke down the bonds between the sugar molecules, so the molecules dissolved more easily.

LIQUIDS

All liquids change shape easily when you pour them from one container to another. Thin liquids pour and flow more easily than thick liquids.

When two different types of liquids are mixed, the molecules of both liquids mingle. If the molecules of one liquid are bigger than the molecules of the other liquid, smaller molecules fit into the spaces among the bigger molecules.

When fine sand is poured into a bucket of stones, the sand fills the spaces among the stones. Liquid molecules work in the same way when mixed.

CLOSE-UP

SURFACE TENSION

Molecules of water pull on each other in all directions. For instance, the water molecules below the surface of a glass of water pull on the water molecules above. This pulls the surface of the water into a tight skin, or film. Some objects can float on the water surface because it is so tight.

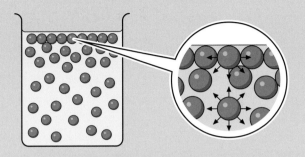

• **Water molecules at the water's surface pull into a tight skin.**

◀ *The molecules in this drop of water are pulling on each other, forcing the drop into a round shape.*

Surface Tension

Surface tension is the result of a force that holds liquid molecules together. For example, molecules of water are strongly attracted to each other and pull together as tightly as they can. That is why small amounts of water form round drops. Surface tension makes the surface of any liquid act as a stretchy covering.

Mixing Liquids

What happens when you mix together different liquids? Try this experiment to find out.

You will need
- 2 tall glasses • washable marker pen
- measuring cup • water • rubbing alcohol
(isopropyl alcohol, available at supermarkets and drug stores)

1 Use the pen to draw a line on the outside of one of the glasses, about one-third of the way from the bottom. Fill the glass with water to the bottom of the mark.

2 Pour the water into the second glass. Then pour more into the first glass, again to the bottom of the mark. Pour this water into the second, unmarked glass.

3 Two measures of water are now in the second glass. Use the pen to mark the water level on the second glass, then empty it.

Molecules of rubbing alcohol are bigger than water molecules. When the water and alcohol were mixed, the smaller water molecules fit into the spaces between the bigger molecules. That is why the alcohol and water mixture took up less room than the two measures of water.

4 Fill the first glass up to the mark with water again. Empty it into the second glass. Now ask an adult to help you fill the first glass up to the mark with rubbing alcohol.

5 Pour the rubbing alcohol from the first glass into the second glass, adding it to the water. What happens to the level of the liquid? Is it above or below the mark that recorded two measures of water?

SAFETY TIP

Ask an adult to help you with this experiment. Rubbing alcohol is safe to touch, but *never* drink it or put it near your eyes or nose.

Creating Bubbles

Bubbles sometimes form on the surface of a liquid. Why? Try this experiment to find out.

1 Put 10 tablespoons of water into the mixing bowl. Add one tablespoon of dishwashing liquid and one teaspoon of corn syrup.

2 Stir the mixture to make a bubble solution. Put three tablespoons of the bubble solution onto the other bowl or plate.

You will need
- water • tablespoon • teaspoon
- dishwashing liquid • mixing bowl
- corn syrup • bowl or plate
- drinking straws • pipe cleaners

3 Using a straw, blow into the solution. Make a bubble. What shape is the bubble? How big of a bubble can you blow?

18

WHAT HAPPENED?

4 Bend and join pipe cleaners to make a cube shape. Attach another pipe cleaner to make a handle.

5 Dip the pipe cleaner cube into the bubble solution in the mixing bowl, then remove it. What happens when you blow through the cube?

The soap molecules in the dishwashing liquid moved between the water molecules. That stopped the water molecules from pulling on each other, which reduced the water's surface tension. Instead of pulling together to form a tight film, they could form into a bubble shape.

Air was trapped inside the bubble. The corn syrup made the bubble last longer because it soaks up water molecules. That stopped the water from evaporating, or turning into a gas.

Try this!

Try to blow another bubble inside the first bubble. Surface tension makes the water molecules in each bubble join to create a shared edge, or side.

GASES

Gases do not have a fixed shape or volume.
They can be forced to fit into smaller spaces,
and they can spread out to fill larger spaces.

There are no bonds between gas molecules, so they are not joined. Instead, the molecules zoom around at high speeds. That is why gases spread out to evenly fill any container. The spaces between molecules in a gas are also large, so the molecules can be squashed together. That is why a gas can be forced into a smaller space.

Gas Pressure

Gas molecules move around inside a container. When gas molecules hit against the sides of a container, they create a force called gas pressure. This pressure can push against other gases, liquids, or even solids.

CLOSE-UP

FIRE EXTINGUISHER

Some fire extinguishers use air pressure in the following way:

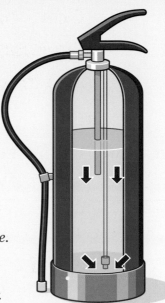

1 *When the extinguisher handle is squeezed, air is quickly released inside the extinguisher. That creates air pressure.*

2 *The air pressure pushes down on a mixture of water and detergent inside the extinguisher.*

3 *The air pressure forces the water and detergent up a tube.*

4 *The water and detergent mixture shoots out of the extinguisher through a nozzle as a jet of foam and water.*

◀ *Air molecules inside a bicycle pump are squashed together when the pump's handle is moved down. This increases the air pressure inside the pump. The pressure pushes air from the pump into the tire, inflating it.*

Mixing Liquids and Gases

When liquids and gases are put in the same container, some of the gas will dissolve in the liquid. They mix because the molecules in both liquids and gases move around.
For instance, a fizzy drink bottle contains both liquid molecules and gas molecules that have mixed together. The gas molecules move between the liquid molecules to make the drink bubbly, or fizzy.

Expanding Gases

How does a gas expand? Find out by trying this activity.

You will need

- small glass jar and large glass jars with lids • 3 feet (1 m) of plastic tubing
- screw cap from a large plastic soda bottle • eyedropper • measuring cup
- 1 Alka-Seltzer™ effervescent tablet
- scissors • modeling clay

1 Ask an adult to drill one hole in the small jar lid and two in the large jar lid. Cut the plastic tubing in half. Push the end of one half through the hole in the small jar lid. Seal any spaces around the hole with modeling clay.

2 Use some modeling clay to stick the bottle cap to the bottom of the small jar (inside the jar). Place an Alka-Seltzer tablet next to it. Use the eyedropper to fill the bottle cap with water. Do not spill any water on the tablet.

3 Carefully screw the lid onto the small jar without spilling any water out of the bottle cap. Push the other end of the tubing that is attached to the small jar into the top of the large jar lid. Seal with clay. Push the other piece of tubing into the second hole in the large jar lid.

22

WHAT HAPPENED?

When the Alka-Seltzer tablet mixed with water it produced a gas called carbon dioxide (CO_2). The carbon dioxide gas expanded, or spread out, to fill the small jar. Some gas pushed up the tubing into the second jar. Gas pressure in the jar increased. The pressure pushed water from the large jar up the second tube and into the measuring cup.

4 Pour water into the large jar until it is two-thirds full. Suck on the end of the tube until you taste the water, then put the tube into the measuring cup. Water will start filling the cup. Lift up the cup until the water stops rising. Water should now fill the tubing from the second jar to the cup.

5 Tilt the small jar until water spills from the cap onto the tablet. Record the level of water in the measuring cup as it changes. Time the change. How much water is displaced? How quickly is the water displaced from the large jar into the cup?

SAFETY TIP

Ask an adult to make the holes in the jars. Make sure that your tubing is washed thoroughly and that no one else puts it in their mouth.

CHANGING STATES

Most substances can change state. This means they can be a solid, a liquid, or a gas. Water is a liquid, but it becomes a solid when it turns to ice. Water becomes a gas when it turns to water vapor.

A change in temperature or pressure can either create or break bonds between atoms and molecules. That causes a change in state.

Solid to Liquid

When a solid heats up, its molecules vibrate more quickly. The vibration causes some of the bonds among the molecules to stretch and break. The molecules can then move around each other, instead of staying close together. The solid becomes liquid.

Liquid to Gas

When a liquid heats up, its molecules move faster. That makes the bonds between some molecules break. These molecules escape from the liquid as gas. The process is called evaporation.

CLOSE-UP

PRESSURE CHANGES

When a gas changes temperature, its pressure changes, too. When a gas is heated in a container, its molecules move around more quickly and bump into each other more often. That increases the gas pressure. When a gas is squashed, or compressed, its temperature and pressure also increase.

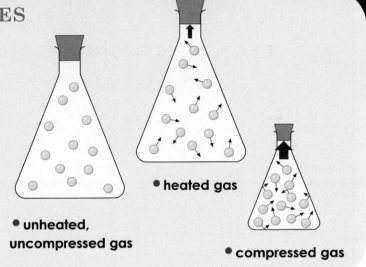

• **unheated, uncompressed gas**

• **heated gas**

• **compressed gas**

◀ *A skater's weight pushes down on the thin blade of his skates. This increases the pressure on the ice just below the skate. The increased pressure lowers the melting point of the ice so that the ice melts slightly. This melting creates a surface of liquid water on which the skates can glide. The water freezes again when the pressure is gone.*

Gas to Liquid and Liquid to Solid

Some changes of state happen when bonds are formed. When a gas cools, its molecules have less energy and move more slowly. Loose bonds start to form among the molecules. When the molecules join up, the substance becomes a liquid. This process is called condensation.

When a liquid cools, its molecules have even less energy. They slow down and tight bonds are formed among them. The molecules link up in a tight, regular pattern, and the liquid becomes a solid.

25

Vapor Trails

Why does a bathroom mirror become steamy when you take a shower? Follow the steps to find out.

1 Pour one-quarter of a cup of water into the bottom of the jar.

2 Turn the glove inside out. Put the candle into the jar. Ask an adult to light the candle. After a few seconds, blow out the candle. Quickly stretch the glove over the jar. The glove should cover the top of the jar.

You will need
- large jar • measuring cup • water
- tealight candle • dishwashing glove

SAFETY TIP

Have an adult light the candle. Always be very careful around the lit candle.

3 After the candle has gone out, put your hand inside the glove. Push your hand into the jar.

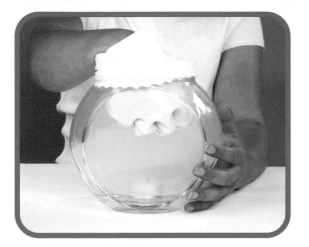

4 Make a fist and pull up the glove as you hold the jar steady with your other hand. Make sure the glove stays tight around the jar. You should see a cloud form inside the jar.

5 Try the experiment again. Remember to have an adult help. This time, put the glove over the top of the jar while the candle is still burning. Take care not to burn yourself. Wait for the candle to go out. Then put your hand in the glove. Make a fist and pull up your hand. What happens?

WHAT HAPPENED?

A cloud formed when you pulled the glove out of the jar. When the glove was pulled up, the water vapor in the jar expanded to fill the extra space. That reduced the pressure in the jar, and the air cooled a little.

The cooler air made the molecules in the water vapor bond. Tiny droplets of water formed on the particles of smoke from the candle. These droplets formed a cloud.

When the glove was pushed back into the jar, the molecules of air inside the jar were forced together. The air pressure and temperature in the jar increased. The droplets turned from liquid back into water vapor.

27

Sliding Ice

Did you know that a piece of thread can pass through a block of ice? Try this experiment to discover why.

You will need

- plastic bottle filled with water
- large metal fork • aluminum foil
- tripod or stand • two heavy books or a weight • thread or string
- ice cube

1 Fill the bottle with water and put on the lid. Place the fork over the tripod. Put the books or weight on the fork. Make sure the fork cannot move.

2 Make a loop in one end of the thread or string. Wrap the other end of the thread or string around the neck of the bottle and tie a knot to hold it in place.

3 Fold the foil into a small square. Put it over the prongs of the fork. Place the ice cube on the foil.

4 Put the loop of the string over the top of the ice cube. The bottle should hang down from the ice cube. Watch what happens.

5 After the string passes partway through the ice cube, lift up the bottle. What do you notice about the ice cube?

WHAT HAPPENED?

When the thread loop was placed over the ice cube, the weight of the bottle put pressure on a small area of the ice cube. The increased pressure also lowered the melting point of the ice, so the ice melted under the string. The area of ice cube under the string melted so that the string could pass partway through it. When you picked up the bottle, the ice cube was attached to the string.

Try this!

Try the experiment again, but this time use a thicker piece of ice. You should find that the thread takes longer to move through a thicker block of ice.

29

GLOSSARY

atoms—Small particles that make up matter. Atoms contain even smaller particles called protons, neutrons, and electrons.

bond—Force that pulls atoms and molecules together or toward each other.

compressed—Forced into a smaller space.

condensation—When a gas cools and turns into a liquid.

dissolve—When the molecules of a solid break away from each other and move between the molecules of a liquid.

electron—Very small, negatively charged particle that moves around the nucleus (center) of an atom.

energy—Ability to do work, such as to make something move or change.

evaporate—To change from a liquid into a gas.

force—Something that can change an object's motion or shape.

gas pressure—The force of gas molecules pushing against other matter.

molecule—Two or more atoms that are joined together.

neutron—Neutral particle in the nucleus of an atom.

nucleus—Center of an atom. The nucleus includes protons and neutrons.

proton—Very small, positively charged particle in an atom's nucleus.

solution—A liquid and a solid that have mixed together.

surface tension—Attraction between liquid molecules that draws them together to create a tight skin over the surface of liquid.

volume—Amount of space that an object takes up.

water vapor—Gas found in air. Water vapor is the gas created when water evaporates.

FURTHER READING

Books

Baldwin, Carol. *States of Matter*. Chicago: Raintree Publishers (2005).

Oxlade, Chris. *Solids, Liquids and Gases.* Chicago: Heinemann Library (2004).

Stille, Darlene R. *Atoms & Molecules: Building Blocks of the Universe.* Minneapolis: Compass Point Books (2007).

Internet Addresses

All About Atoms
http://education.jlab.org/atomtour

States of Matter
http://www.chem4kids.com/files/matter_intro.html

The Atoms Family
http://www.miamisci.org/af/sln

INDEX

A
atom, 4–5, 6, 8, 24

B
bubbles, 7, 18–19

C
condensation, 25
cutting, 9, 10–11

D
dissolving, 9, 12–13, 21

E
electrons, 5
evaporation, 24

G
gas, 6–7, 19, 20–21, 22–23,
   24–25, 27
gas pressure, 20–21, 23, 25

L
liquid, 6–7, 9, 12–13, 14–15, 16–17,
   18–19, 20–21, 24–25, 27

M
mixing, 16–17, 21
molecules, 4–5, 6–7, 8–9, 11, 13,
   14–15, 17, 19, 20–21, 24–25, 27

N
neutrons, 5
nucleus, 5

P
protons, 5

S
shaping, 9, 10–11
solid, 6–7, 8–9, 12–13, 20, 24–25
states of matter, 6–7, 24–25
surface tension, 15, 19

V
volume, 9, 20

W
water vapor, 24, 27